GOD Raised Me

"The ABC's Of God's Promise to Me"

Written By: April Finley

First printing October 2024

Library of Congress Cataloging-in-Publication Data

Paperback ISBN: 979-8-218-53468-4

Published by Royal Palms Publishing, LLC
www.royalpalmspublishing.com

Printed in the U.S.A.

Table Of Contents

This book highlights key scriptures and personal anecdotes that illustrate how God's promises have reshaped my life. It is my hope that readers will find inspiration and encouragement in my story, realizing that God's promises are not just for me, but for everyone who seeks His presence. As I reflect on my journey from pain to purpose, I invite you to join me in exploring the ABCs of God's promises, and to discover the abundant life that awaits you through faith and surrender.

Intro

When I wrote my first book "Healing a Holy Heart, A walk through the emotions of my life", I didn't realize that that was the beginning of my fullness of surrendering to our father. See before you start the healing process. You must acknowledge, hold yourself accountable and surrender all the burdens that you don't even have control of. So, I was ready to give my life to Christ, not halfway, but all the way no longer being lukewarm in the world. No, I'm not perfect, but I am willing and because I love the Lord and I wanted a stronger relationship with our father, it was time to let go and let God. I got baptized on March 12, 2023, and that was the beginning of my walk with Christ Jesus. I knew something was different, but it was almost like I was being trained and raised all over again, but in a different light now when I look back, it was a rebirth. Yes, my parents birthed me, but I realize now how God was raising me, teaching me and maturing me for who he had called me to be. A child of God, a servant of God, a disciple maker, and a leader in the kingdom. So, in the chapters of this book, the ABC's of God 's promise to me you will see how he restored me and-transform right before my own eyes. Just know if he did it for me, he can do it for you. You're never too old or too young.

And most importantly, you have a lot more time in front of you than you have behind you if you believe and have faith in the promise of God.

Chapter 1

ABUNDANCE

In my past, immersed in worldly ways, I never recognized the abundance in my life—if I had experienced it at all. All I knew were feelings of abandonment, abuse, aggression, and anger. Living in such an environment day in and day out, it became nearly impossible to see anything good emerging from that darkness. I accepted this harsh reality as my identity, believing that it was simply who I was meant to be.

However, everything began to shift when I turned to the Scriptures. Reading the book of Genesis, I was particularly struck by the story of Abram, who was called to leave his father, family, and home to venture into an unfamiliar land, trusting in a promise he couldn't yet see. I felt a deep connection to Abram's journey. In 2018, the Holy Spirit prompted me to go to Texas. At the time, I didn't fully understand why; it was just a feeling that pulled at my heart. Admittedly,

I wasn't obedient right away, but four years later, I finally stepped out in faith, despite my fears.

The journey was anything but easy, but once I arrived in Texas, it was as if the Holy Spirit was confirming that I was exactly where I needed to be. I experienced a profound sense of rightness, yet I also felt a wave of discomfort. Being in a new place, away from what was familiar, was challenging. But then I heard God's voice urging me to "be prepared to be comfortable with being uncomfortable." That was the first moment I cried upon hearing the Holy Spirit; His voice was soothing, clear, clean, and direct.

Attending church every Sunday became a priority for me, something that had not always been the case in my life. In the past, I had gone to church when invited, but often it felt more like an obligation than a calling. This time, however, I felt genuinely led to participate, even though it was uncomfortable for me. I grappled with social anxiety, feeling isolated from people, places, and activities. I found it difficult to engage with those who exuded love, joy, peace, and the overall spirit-led energy that I longed for. I knew I wasn't quite there yet, but I was on a journey toward that fulfillment.

One of the pivotal moments in my journey was attending a women's group at church called the Life Group. Every Sunday morning, we would gather to discuss Scripture and study God's Word. One verse that resonated deeply with me came from

Deuteronomy 8:17-18, which emphasizes that the abundance of life is a gift from God—not something that can be earned or deserved. This revelation made me delve deeper into the Word, awakening me to the fact that I had been gifted with the abundance of life. Simply uttering the word "abundance" stirred something profound within my soul. My spirit had always been in communion with God, but my soul— where all my emotions resided—began to shift as I embraced this new understanding.

As I started to internalize what abundance truly meant, I noticed a significant transformation. The taste of the word "abundance" on my lips felt refreshing, almost sweet, and I welcomed it wholeheartedly. I recognized that I was moving away from the confines of my past and stepping into a life rich in the promises of God.

ISAIAH 53:5

"For I, the LORD your God, hold your right hand; it is I who say to you, 'Fear not, I am the one who helps you."

Chapter 2

BLESSING

I remember thinking, why don't I have blessings in my life? It couldn't possibly be a blessing being a parentless child with a child of my own, navigating the harsh reality of homelessness, feeling the weight of mental isolation pressing down on me. My relationships were defined by trauma bonding, each connection fraught with pain and confusion. I often felt uncomfortable in my own skin, battling the uncertainty of some days where I went without meals, and others where I lacked the essential things I believed I needed to survive. In those moments of desperation, the only question lingering in my mind was, "Why can't I have a blessing? Why hasn't God blessed me yet?" The thought crept in that perhaps I didn't deserve a blessing, that I was somehow unworthy of the good that others seemed to receive so effortlessly. These were the thoughts that echoed in my mind throughout my formative years, a constant dialogue of doubt and longing.

Eventually, I reached a point of exhaustion, where I simply stopped asking. It felt futile, as if my pleas were falling on deaf ears. I began to internalize the belief that I was navigating this world alone, that I had to rely solely on myself for any semblance of support or solace. In that realization, I understood that I had the power to be my own biggest blessing. I learned to cultivate resilience within myself, to find strength in my struggles, and to recognize the small victories in each day. I started to appreciate the moments of clarity that broke through the fog of despair, the fleeting instances of joy that reminded me I was still alive and capable. In nurturing my own spirit, I discovered that sometimes the greatest blessing comes not from external sources but from within—an awakening of self-love and acceptance that I had long overlooked.

Numbers 6:24-26 - "The Lord bless you and keep you; the Lord make his face to shine upon you and be gracious to you; the Lord lift up his countenance upon you and give you peace."

Chapter 3

CHOICES AND CHANCES, CARES AND COMFORT

I'm not trying to speak as if I'm all holier than thou. Rather, I share my journey with you from a place of authenticity, shaped by experiences that profoundly changed me after I gave my life to Christ. My hope is to convey this with confidence and gratitude, knowing that if I had embraced these truths earlier in my life, my path might have been steadier. Yet, I realize now that every hardship and challenge I faced was necessary for my growth, leading me to this moment where I can testify about my spiritual journey with you wonderful souls.

One of the most significant lessons I've learned is that God gives us both choices and chances. Life is filled with walls, mistakes, and missteps, and through it all, He patiently waits for us, even when we should be the ones waiting on Him. It's a beautiful, poignant dance of faith and surrender. When we reach the point of saying, "I'm ready," He is there, extending His hands toward us, welcoming us with open arms, ready to walk alongside us. I have felt this deeply in my own life. There were times when I made poor decisions, fought my own battles, and chose my own poison. Yet, in moments of desperation, when I cried out to God, admitting that I needed Him more than ever amidst situations that felt beyond my understanding, He answered me.

Over the years, I asked God for many things. Some blessings came swiftly, almost like gifts wrapped just for me. However, many others seemed delayed, which often left me anxious and eager to take matters into my own hands. I didn't recognize at the time that those delays were part of a divine test, a way for me to build my testimony. God knew there would come a day when I would finally say yes to Him, choosing to place Him at the center of everything I do. Ironically, I didn't realize that my life was already intertwined with His plans; everything about me is, after all, God's business. Yet, while I was busy trying to control my own narrative, I learned that everything God orchestrates is not mine to dictate.

Reflecting on this now brings a smile to my face, realizing how misguided I was. But the moment I chose Him, after countless chances to turn back, something miraculous happened: He cared for me and comforted me in ways I had never experienced before. Until I fully surrendered my life to God, I had never truly felt safe. When I say that He gives us chances, choices, cares, and comforts, I mean it wholeheartedly. His promises are real, and I stand as a testament to the fact that He keeps them. Reading His Word reassures me of His faithfulness, and I can confidently share my experience as proof of His enduring love and commitment to those who seek Him with open hearts.

1 PETER 5:6-7

"Humble yourselves, therefore, under the mighty hand of God so that at the proper time He may exalt you, casting all your anxieties on Him, because He cares for you."

Chapter 4

DELIVERANCE

The very word embodies the long journey it took for me to truly experience it. I initially thought deliverance was solely about external circumstances, but I soon recognized that I needed liberation from within as well—from my own mental struggles, anxiety, and the weight of depression. For too long, I found myself trapped in a cycle of overthinking, sabotaging my own happiness and progress. The enemy was relentless, trying to diminish my spirit, yet the beautiful truth is that God was always there, anchoring me even when I was unaware of His presence.

God serves as our intercessor, provider, and protector. In moments where it felt like the enemy had me in a chokehold, I realize now that God had me in a stronghold. The enemy may have tried to invade my mind and heart, but ultimately, he never had true access to me. The real battle was within, a struggle of self-sabotage that I had to confront. When I reflect on how God delivered me, saved me, and set me free, I can't help but give Him all the praise and worship He deserves.

Sitting on this side of deliverance feels like taking a breath of fresh air after being submerged for too long. I remember the days when I would walk into the doctor's office, my blood pressure soaring to alarming heights—197/119, and sometimes even higher. Those visits were filled with anxiety, each number on the monitor a reminder of the internal chaos I was battling. But now, each check-up reveals perfect blood pressure, a testament to the transformation that has taken place within me. This change is not merely medical; it is spiritual. I share this not just to celebrate my health but to illustrate how surrendering my burdens, casting all my cares and anxieties upon the Lord, has led to my deliverance. God kept His promise to me.

Now, I am able to sit still and wait on the Lord with a newfound peace. Every decision I make, I consult with my Father first, for He is my answer to every question that life throws my way. When people ask me, "Why do you?" my answer is God. When they inquire, "What do you?" my response is still God. "When do you?"— the answer remains God. "Where do you?"—once again, it's God. And when they ask, "How do you?" the answer is clear: my God.

I trust Him wholeheartedly because He has delivered me from everything that sought to come against me.

For this, I am forever grateful. This journey of deliverance is ongoing, and each day is a reminder of His grace and faithfulness. In recognizing that He is the source of my strength and peace, I find joy in the simplicity of turning to Him for guidance, comfort, and love. My deliverance is not just a moment in time; it's a continuous path of growth and healing, and I embrace it with open arms, knowing that God will always hold me close.

PHILIPPIANS
2:3-4

"Do nothing from selfish ambition or conceit, but in humility count others more significant than yourselves. Let each of you look not only to his own interests, but also to the interests of others."

Chapter 5

ETERNAL LIFE

I remember as a child, and even in my younger years, grappling with a profound fear of death. Living in the world without a strong understanding of my faith, I often found myself consumed by thoughts of dying. Who wants to face such a finality? My mind would race with dark imaginations—dying in my sleep, drowning in a pool, or even being shot and bleeding out. The very thought of death became a source of paralyzing fear, leading me to numb myself to its reality. I missed many funerals of those close to me—family and friends—because I conditioned my mind to shut down in the face of loss. In hindsight, I realize this was a selfish response, driven by my lack of understanding. The enemy seized upon my fear, conditioning my thoughts and silencing God's voice in my heart, which left me unable to hear the messages of hope and comfort He was sending.

But then I discovered the promise of eternal life. The scripture illuminated my understanding, revealing that the Holy Spirit lives within us and never dies.

This promise of eternal life is not just a fleeting notion; it is an everlasting gift from God. When I came to understand that my life was formed in my mother's womb and that my earthly journey would continue in heaven, I felt an overwhelming sense of gratitude. That realization was one of the greatest gifts I could ever ask for. It allowed me to set aside my fears and let God consume my thoughts and emotions. The closer I draw to Him, the stronger our relationship becomes, and with that, my faith deepens. I hold onto the assurance that I will experience eternal life.

Looking back over my life, I reflect on the countless times I prayed, asking God to bring my mother back. I wrestled with questions about why He had to take her and others I loved. But now, with maturity and spiritual understanding, I sit with God in prayer, seeking His forgiveness for those questions I once asked in pain. I have come to trust God deeply, knowing that everything He does is purposeful. As much as I love and miss my mother in this physical realm, I find solace in the knowledge that she has eternal life and is with God. Her unwavering love for the Lord assures me of her place in His presence.

I can rejoice now, giving God all the praise for the plans He has for my life. The understanding of eternal life transforms my grief into gratitude. Instead of being shackled by fear and loss, I am uplifted by the hope of reunion in heaven. Each day, as I grow in my faith, I find comfort in the promise that death is not the end but rather a transition into a glorious eternity.

This perspective has reshaped my relationship with life and death, allowing me to embrace the journey ahead with a heart full of trust and love for my Savior.

PSALM 62:1-2

"Truly my soul
finds rest in God;
my salvation
comes from him.
Truly he is my
rock and my
salvation; he is my
fortress, I will
never be shaken."

Chapter 6

FAITH AND FAITHFULNESS

Faith and faithfulness are deeply intertwined concepts that profoundly affect our relationship with God. While God is unchanging— " the same yesterday, today, and forever" (Hebrews 13:8)—our understanding of faith can evolve. Each day, God fulfills His promises to me, reinforcing the notion that He is indeed a faithful Father. Yet, when faced with the challenge of differentiating between mere faith and true faithfulness, I found myself at a crossroads. Initially, during my healing journey, I believed that simply having faith was sufficient. Each morning, I would wake up, expressing gratitude and belief in God, but I soon realized that my commitment to Him was not as deep as it should have been.

I was still attached to worldly desires—those things, people, and places that God had intentionally distanced me from. My soul craved these distractions, which prevented me from fully committing to God. I wanted to be close to Him, but I wasn't fully surrendering my heart. This lack of complete faithfulness meant that I was holding back parts of myself, and it took a spiritual awakening for me to understand the depth of this challenge. God desires not just our belief but our unwavering faith—faith that surpasses His promises, which are always fulfilled.

The Bible tells us that faith as small as a mustard seed can move mountains, but God challenges us to examine our faithfulness alongside our faith. I realized that having faith in God is one thing, but being faithful to Him requires a deeper commitment. It meant prioritizing my relationship with Him above all else. I found myself retreating to prayer, seeking guidance and clarity, asking God to help me surrender my will and desires. I understood that I must continuously surrender, again and again, until I truly grasp this lesson.

As I processed these revelations, I felt a weight lifted from my shoulders, prompting an emotional release. In my past relationships, I often had faith that they would succeed, yet I was not faithful to God in those situations. I placed my trust in people rather than seeking God's wisdom and guidance. This misalignment taught me that true faithfulness means consulting God for my needs and desires rather than relying on others.

Through this journey, God made it clear that He should be at the center of my life. When I turned to those I had once relied on, I discovered that they were no longer present, which shattered my reliance on external validation. This experience forced me to confront my faith and trust what was within me rather than what I could see. As the scripture reminds us, we must "walk by faith and not by sight."

Ultimately, I learned that my faith must align with my faithfulness. Faith represents my belief in God's promises, while faithfulness embodies my loyalty and commitment to Him. It's essential to reflect on whether our faith is truly aligned with our faithfulness. Are we putting our trust in what we see, or are we leaning into the spirit that resides within us? These are questions we must ask ourselves as we navigate our spiritual journeys, reminding us that faith is not just a belief but a commitment to living in accordance with God's will.

ISAIAH 41:10 (NIV)

"So do not fear, for I am with you; do not be dismayed, for I am your God. I will strengthen you and help you; I will uphold you with my righteous right hand."

Chapter 7

GUIDANCE

Throughout the years, much of what I've learned about life has been inherited from the women in my family—my mother, my aunts, and the close friends who surrounded me. If you're unfamiliar with my story, it's essential to understand the profound loss I experienced at a young age. When I was just eight years old, my father was murdered, thrusting me into a world of confusion and grief. By the time I reached 17, I faced another devastating blow with the passing of my mother due to breast, liver, and colon cancer, all while I was navigating the complexities of young motherhood with a one-year-old daughter to care for. It's safe to say that I felt utterly lost, devoid of guidance in a world that suddenly felt overwhelmingly large and unwelcoming.

I had no one to walk me through the trials of motherhood or the challenges of adulthood; I felt as though I was wandering through life without a map. This sense of isolation led me to believe that I was learning everything the hard way, experiencing trial and error with each step I took. My journey was marked by mistakes—many of which I can't erase from my memory, yet I wouldn't want to even if I could. Those experiences, steeped in hurt, anger, and pain, shaped me into who I am today, even before I committed my life to Christ. Some might have labeled my actions as reckless, but in truth, I was simply trying to navigate adulthood without any guidance, thrust into responsibilities I hadn't asked for and felt ill-prepared to handle.

However, everything changed when I surrendered my life to God. As I began to immerse myself in His Word, I discovered a source of guidance I had overlooked for so long. Scripture became my compass, illuminating my path and providing the direction I desperately needed. Psalm 119:105 resonates deeply with me: "Thy word is a lamp unto my feet and a light unto my path." It was through these verses that I learned about God's unwavering presence in every aspect of our lives, as emphasized in Romans 8:28, where God assures us that He works everything together for our good and His glory. And then there's Jeremiah 29:11, a beautiful reminder that God has a plan for each of us; yet, we must be willing to seek it out.

Before I opened the Bible, I lived in a constant state of survival, fighting to keep my head above water for 28 long years. Despite my struggles, God was my anchor all along, holding me steady and preventing me from drowning in despair. He knew I had a purpose, even when I was oblivious to it myself. This realization has transformed my perspective; I now understand that trusting the process with God is crucial. Allowing Him to guide me has been a revelation, providing a sense of peace and direction that I had long sought.

As I continue on this journey, I recognize that God is not only my protector but also the one who holds my hand through every trial and triumph. With His guidance, I am confident that the rewards awaiting me at the end of this race will far exceed anything I could have imagined. Each day, I am reminded that if God has been faithful to me in my struggles, He will be equally faithful to you in yours. Embrace His guidance and trust that your path is being illuminated, leading you toward a future filled with hope and purpose.

1 THESSALONIANS
5:16-18

"Rejoice always,
pray without
ceasing, give
thanks in all
circumstances; for
this is the will of
God in Christ
Jesus for you."

Chapter 8

HOPE

Hope is the lifeline that sustains me every single day. It's a profound feeling that transcends mere words; it's a deep-seated assurance within my soul. This isn't just wishful thinking or a fleeting desire; it's a steadfast hope rooted in my faith that God will provide, protect, cover, and love me in ways I cannot even fully comprehend. I can speak to this hope with authority and grace, knowing that it is not misplaced. Throughout my journey, I have witnessed how God keeps His promises, and I am a living testament to that truth. Every time I have placed my hope in Him, He has delivered, never allowing me to falter or fall into despair.

God has never let me down. In fact, He has been my unwavering support, a constant reminder that I am never alone. Each day, I watch as He transforms me—physically, emotionally, and spiritually. When I look in the mirror, I see the evidence of this transformation; I see the growth and change that embodies everything I have hoped for. It's as if each new day brings a fresh opportunity to become the person I was always meant to be.

There were times when I felt lost, yearning to surrender to God but unsure of how to do so. In those moments of desperation, I would cry out to Him, pleading, "God, I hope to experience the love, joy, and peace that You have promised." And time and again, my Father has answered with a resounding "yes." He has led me into unfamiliar territory, pushing me beyond my comfort zone to experience the fullness of His presence. This journey into the unknown has not always been easy, but my trust in Him has made it bearable.

Because I trust Him, my requests have become more consistent, grounded in a faith that has been nurtured over time. I've learned that hope is not just a passive waiting; it's an active engagement with God's promises. With each prayer, I am reaffirmed in my belief that He is working all things for my good. My hope is now intertwined with my faith, creating a powerful force that propels me forward each day.

This hope reassures me that no matter the challenges I face, God is with me every step of the way, guiding and uplifting me. It reminds me that His plans for me are filled with purpose and that every struggle is part of a greater story. In embracing this hope, I find strength and courage to navigate the uncertainties of life, knowing that with God, I am always moving towards something beautiful.

PSALM
34:4-5, 8

"I sought the LORD, and He answered me and delivered me from all my fears. Those who look to Him are radiant, and their faces shall never be ashamed. Oh, taste and see that the LORD is good! Blessed is the man who takes refuge in Him!."

Chapter 9

INSPIRATION

Throughout this journey, I have been surrounded by an abundance of inspiration, a divine presence that constantly uplifts and guides me. I am immensely grateful to the Lord above for His declarations, for sending exactly what I need, when I need it, and in the precise manner that resonates with my soul. There's a profound sense of relief that comes with relinquishing control over the chaos of the world— surrendering everything to God feels liberating. This act of surrender has opened my heart and mind to the inspiration He provides, transforming my spiritual walk into a rich tapestry of teachings and learnings that continually nourish my spirit.

There are moments when I am unsure of when to move or how to take the next step, and it is during these times that God intervenes. He sends someone into my life, reveals a sign, or speaks directly to my heart, awakening a sense of urgency and motivation within me. This kind of inspiration is rare and precious; it's the kind that transcends ordinary encouragement. I have come to realize that the people who inspire me are often guided by God's hand, and I am reminded that the Holy Spirit is at work in our lives 24/7. If only we could quiet our own voices and distractions, we would hear Him speak more clearly.

As I write and share my experiences, I've begun to understand just how deeply God has inspired me. He has allowed me to prophesy over my own life, speaking things into existence that are now unfolding right before my eyes. Even in this moment, as I sit here writing and expressing my thoughts, I recognize that these are manifestations of the hopes and dreams I once articulated, sometimes without even realizing God was listening. I can assure you, He heard every word, and He has been showing me signs and visions about my next book. Many have been asking, "When is the next one coming out?" I would often respond that it was on the way, yet I struggled to find the focus to complete it.

But God orchestrated my circumstances in such a way that reignited my spirit, urging me to write and share the messages of His promises. I feel motivated to put pen to paper, to explore the depths of what He has revealed to me, and to share these insights with others. My mission is not just about my journey; it's about conveying the alphabet of God's promises to all who will listen, reminding everyone that these assurances are available to them as well.

Ultimately, God is my greatest source of inspiration. He is the foundation upon which everything else is built, the driving force that leads people into my life through divine connections. These connections inspire me to continue doing His work and motivate me to be an inspiration to others. It's essential to acknowledge that all the glory belongs to Him. Therefore, I encourage everyone to silence their own voices, quiet their thoughts, and allow God to consume them. In doing so, you will invite His divine inspiration into your life, transforming your journey in ways you never thought possible. Let His voice guide you, and you will discover a wellspring of creativity, purpose, and hope that fuels your spirit.

DEUTERONOMY
31:8-9

"The Lord himself goes before you and will be with you; he will never leave you nor forsake you. Do not be afraid; do not be discouraged."

Chapter 10

JOY

So here I am, basking in everything I have asked for—the joy I longed for is finally becoming a tangible part of my life. I am learning to find joy even amid my troubles, embracing the truth that "troubles don't last always; joy comes in the morning." This belief has taken root in my heart more than ever before. When challenges arise, and they often do—because let's face it, I never really had control over my circumstances—I remind myself to laugh. It's a way of coping, a recognition of the absurdity of trying to figure everything out on my own.

In the past, I would scramble to solve problems, convinced that I had all the answers. However, time and again, God would show up right on time, flipping the script on my worries. It could be something as simple as a timely financial blessing or a sudden postponement of a due date that eased my stress. Reflecting on those moments, I realize that I didn't always give Him the praise and honor He deserved for making a way out of no way. But now, as I deepen my understanding of God through His Word and experience His presence like never before, I find myself less concerned about worldly troubles. Every day I wake up is a gift, an opportunity to embrace the joy that God provides.

Throughout my journey to this point, I have often looked back at the hardships I faced. Initially, they seemed insurmountable, but now I see them as tests that shaped me. During those tough times, my greatest source of joy was my children. God blessed me with them, knowing how deeply I love and cherish family. They became my motivation to keep moving forward, my anchors during turbulent times. Being a mother has not been without its challenges, but I have learned to hold myself accountable, recognizing the importance of acknowledging my past struggles. This self-awareness is crucial in breaking the generational curses that have loomed over my family.

I've come to embrace the idea that I am open to correction. When you're on a journey and feel isolated, it's easy to believe you've done everything on your own, and it can be hard to accept guidance from others. However, God has humbled me significantly. Now, I find myself living in the present moment, fully experiencing the joy that God has imparted to me. I am no longer fixated on my past mistakes or overly anxious about what the future holds. Instead, I am here, fully present, and immersed in the beauty of now.

This newfound perspective allows me to rejoice in each day, recognizing that joy is not just an emotion but a choice—a choice to see the good in every situation and to trust that God is working in my life, even when I can't immediately see the results. I am grateful for the lessons learned, the joy discovered in the journey, and the continuous growth that comes from trusting God. Each moment is a reminder that joy is a gift from Him, and I am committed to receiving it wholeheartedly, celebrating the life He has blessed me with.

JOHN 14:27

"Peace I leave with you; my peace I give you. I do not give to you as the world gives. Do not let your hearts be troubled and do not be afraid."

Chapter 11

KINDNESS

Colossians 3:12 beautifully states, "Therefore, as God's chosen people, holy and dearly loved, clothe yourselves with compassion, kindness, humility, gentleness, and patience." At first glance, this verse seems straightforward, almost simplistic. I used to think of kindness merely as a polite gesture or a nice word. However, since surrendering my life to Christ, I have come to understand that kindness encompasses so much more—it's about embodying Christ-like qualities and representing His love in everything I do.

Since I made this commitment, I can genuinely say I see myself differently. There's a noticeable change in how I perceive my own presence, and I've become aware that others notice it too. In the past, I often kept my head down, avoiding attention and blending into the background. But now, as I embrace my identity in Christ, I walk into rooms with a newfound confidence and purpose. I want to shine as a light for others, reflecting the love and grace that God has poured into my life. This transformation inspires me to treat others as God treats me—with kindness, love, and respect.

Being kind is particularly challenging when faced with unkindness from others. Yet, I have come to realize that kindness is a choice, one that I am determined to make regardless of how others behave. God has called me to be a leader, and I strive to lead by example. I refuse to let someone else's negativity dictate my actions or diminish the kindness I strive to embody. Instead, I focus on being a source of inspiration and encouragement for those around me, aiming to be a living testament to the teachings of Jesus Christ.

It hasn't been an easy journey to reach this point; it has taken time, reflection, and a deep commitment to grow in my faith. But I am steadfast in my determination to remain rooted in kindness, regardless of external circumstances. I understand that leaving a positive impression on others is vital, and I want to reflect the same impression that God has left on my heart. Kindness is not merely an act; it's an integral part of my spiritual journey and a central theme in Scripture.

Every opportunity I have to be kind is a chance to demonstrate God's love in action. I am learning that kindness is not just a virtue; it's a powerful expression of our faith. By choosing to be kind, I contribute to a ripple effect that can touch lives and inspire others to do the same. This is one of the most significant lessons God has taught me, and I embrace it wholeheartedly. I am committed to cultivating kindness in my heart and sharing it with the world, knowing that in doing so, I am fulfilling my purpose and reflecting the character of Christ.

ROMANS 5:5

"And hope does not put us to shame, because God's love has been poured out into our hearts through the Holy Spirit, who has been given to us."

Chapter 12

LOVE

I'm filled with excitement as I navigate through the ABC's of God's promises to me, and one of the most profound lessons I've learned on this journey is about love. Over the past two and a half years, I have embarked on a spiritual journey that has transformed my understanding of this powerful emotion. At 47 years old, I find it somewhat embarrassing to admit that the deep, unconditional love I always yearned for didn't truly manifest in my life until I was 45. While many might point to the love of their children as a source of joy, I've come to realize that love looks vastly different when viewed through the lens of hurt and pain compared to the clarity of a healed heart.

For a long time, my love for my children was clouded by my own struggles. In my pain, I found it challenging to fully engage with their emotions or to provide the comfort they needed. I often didn't listen to them as I should have, because I simply didn't know how. My experiences had taught me a distorted version of love that was intertwined with my own unresolved issues. Even in relationships, I mistook infatuation or lust for love, believing I was in love when it was often a shallow imitation of true connection.

Now, through my spiritual journey and the time spent in communion with God, I have come to understand the true definition of agape love—an unconditional, selfless love that reflects the very essence of God's heart. This transformation has allowed me to revisit my love for my children. Today, I love them fiercely, to the point where I would do anything to protect them. If anyone ever threatened them, I would stand in the way without hesitation, willing to do whatever it takes to keep them safe.

In past relationships, I thought I loved deeply, yet I often turned a blind eye to behaviors that God was trying to reveal to me. I accepted what I thought was love, but now, I find myself in a profound relationship with God where I experience agape love in its purest form. I can confidently say that I love myself and recognize my worth. This newfound understanding of love empowers me to release my children back to God, trusting in His divine plan for their lives rather than trying to control their paths.

God has shown me that my role as a praying mother is far more significant than any material possessions or superficial comforts I might offer. I've come to learn that overly indulging my children can actually hinder their growth. This revelation has shaped my spiritual journey, guiding me to follow His Word. Though I sometimes struggle to stay on course, I cling to the promise that God will provide and protect.

Through the agape love that God has bestowed upon me, I am now able to extend that same love to others—my brothers and sisters in Christ. I can express my love confidently, knowing that I mean it with sincerity. This divine love fosters patience, understanding, and a willingness to listen. I am learning to acknowledge my shortcomings and hold myself accountable. I am not perfect, but I am committed to growing and improving.

What better teacher could I have than our Father and His Word? Each day, I strive to embody the love that I have received from God, knowing that it is this love that will guide me in my relationships and allow me to impact the lives of those around me. This journey has been transformative, and I look forward to continuing to grow in love, inspired by the ultimate example of love that God has given us.

PSALM 116:1-2

"I love the Lord,
for he heard my
voice; he heard
my cry for mercy.
Because he
turned his ear to
me, I will call on
him as long as I
live."

Chapter 13

MIRACULOUS

What a mighty God we serve! His power and strength are beyond comprehension. Our God is truly miraculous; when I say He can change circumstances in the blink of an eye, I speak from personal experience. I want to share a story that serves as a testament to His incredible grace and ability to transform our lives in ways we could never imagine.

When I moved to Texas, my journey began in an Airbnb, where I lived for about two months. I arrived in June, but it wasn't until August 2022 that I finally moved into my new home. This experience is detailed in my first book, and it serves as a powerful reminder of God's miraculous nature for those who truly know Him. I vividly remember the moment I transitioned from living in temporary housing to finally sitting in my own home. After navigating countless obstacles and red tape, I was finally able to breathe deeply, sitting on my bed, surrounded by boxes that I was trying to sort through and organize.

In the corner of my room stood a large mirror. When I sat at the foot of my bed, I would often look into it and feel a sense that I needed to move it; I didn't like the way it faced me and my bed. However, I didn't act on that feeling right away. Instead, I found myself opening the mail that had accumulated during my move. Among the letters, one from the mortgage company caught my attention. I had been anxiously waiting for news about my loan, and I was puzzled by the lengthy process; I had expected to be in my home much sooner than this.

As I opened the letter, I was met with confusion and disbelief. The letter informed me that my loan application for the house I was already living in had been denied. How could this be? I was sitting there in the very home I was being denied a loan for! Just moments later, I opened another letter from the mortgage company, which also contained a denial—this time regarding assistance for my closing costs. It was surreal to read these letters while physically occupying the house they claimed I had no financial right to.

In that moment of confusion, I was reminded of God's promise that sometimes we may face delays, but we are never truly denied. God, in His miraculous way, was revealing to me the difference between what is possible in our human understanding and what He can accomplish when we place our faith in Him. I was now sitting in the house that I had been denied a loan for, a clear demonstration of God's power to change situations that seem impossible.

I don't know about you, but my experience solidifies my faith in a God who works miracles. He can turn any situation around, bringing good from what seems like defeat. He did it for me, and I am fully confident that He can and will do it for you, too. This experience has left me in awe of how God's plans often surpass our expectations, reminding me that with faith, we can witness the miraculous unfold in our lives.

JEREMIAH
29:11

"For I know the plans I have for you, declares the Lord, plans to prosper you and not to harm you, plans to give you hope and a future."

Chapter 14

NOBLE

This one may be short and sweet, but it carries profound significance. Our God is noble and truly worthy of all praise, not just for what He does, but for who He is at His very essence. His nobility is rooted in His character, His limitless love, and the grace He extends to us daily. When we consider where He comes from—the Creator of the universe, the Alpha and Omega—we are reminded of His majesty and power. He is not just any deity; He is the King of Kings and Lord of Lords, holding authority over all things.

Moreover, His noble nature is reflected in the countless ways He has intervened in our lives. He has fought our battles, provided for our needs, and offered us redemption and salvation. Each act of kindness, each moment of mercy, and every ounce of grace He bestows upon us are affirmations of His worthiness. We praise Him not only for the miracles and blessings we receive but for the very fact that He cares for us deeply and knows us intimately.

To acknowledge God's nobility is to recognize His honor and integrity, qualities that are often lacking in the world around us. In a society that can sometimes prioritize superficiality, it's refreshing to be reminded of the depth of His character and the authenticity of His love. It inspires us to reflect those qualities in our own lives, striving to be honorable and noble in our actions and relationships.

Thus, this chapter may be brief, but it encapsulates a profound truth: our God deserves our praise, not just for what He has done for us, but for the very nature of who He is. His nobility is a reminder that we are called to emulate these qualities in our own lives. So let us lift our voices in gratitude and adoration, recognizing that our God is indeed worthy of every ounce of praise we can offer. That's it—that's the chapter! In its simplicity, it invites us to dwell on the greatness of our God and to live lives that reflect His nobility.

Chapter 15

OBEDIENCE

Obedience in the spiritual realm is profoundly different from the kind of obedience we often encounter in the world. In the secular world, we tend to navigate life according to our desires, often overwhelmed by confusion, distractions, disappointments, and a general lack of self-control. We chase after our whims, believing we know what's best for ourselves, but this often leads us into chaos. In stark contrast, spiritual obedience is rooted in a singular truth—the truth that is found in the Word of God. This truth becomes our guiding light, illuminating our paths, especially when we cultivate a strong relationship with the Holy Spirit.

In my own journey, I struggled significantly with obedience. I often found myself engaging in self-sabotage, a pattern that stemmed from my trials and tribulations. God, in His infinite wisdom, would wave the metaphorical red and white flags in front of me, signaling what was meant for me and what was not.

Yet, despite these divine warnings, I would pursue what I thought I wanted, often ignoring the signs that pointed me away from darkness. It was as if I had convinced myself that I had control over my circumstances, even when that control was leading me deeper into a shadowy abyss.

For me, the more I acted on my own understanding and made decisions without consulting God, the darker my life became. However, everything shifted when I began to grasp the importance of the Word and foster a relationship with God. I learned to pray before making decisions, seeking His guidance rather than relying on my flawed reasoning. This practice brought light into my life, illuminating the right paths and helping me avoid the pitfalls I had previously fallen into. God became my guiding light, showing me the way when my own efforts only led to destruction.

I recognize that many people express a desire to turn back time and redo certain choices in their lives. However, I can honestly say I wouldn't change anything about my past. Every experience, even the painful ones, has been a learning opportunity that shaped who I am today. Most importantly, these experiences have led me to establish one of the most significant relationships of my life—my relationship with God. I could have sought healing in another relationship, but I would have only brought more trauma and hurt into my life. Instead, I am grateful that God allowed me to listen, to be still, and to embrace obedience to His Word.

Now, I am discovering that obedience is essential in every aspect of our lives. It's not just a spiritual exercise; it's a way of living that impacts our relationships and choices. I am thankful for the lessons I've learned in the physical realm about obedience, as they reinforce the spiritual truths God has instilled in me. By practicing obedience, I am not only honoring God but also paving the way for a life filled with peace, purpose, and fulfillment. Each day, I strive to align my actions with His will, knowing that true freedom and joy come from living in obedience to the One who knows what's best for me.

ROMANS
15:13 (NIV)

"May the God of hope fill you with all joy and peace as you trust in Him, so that you may overflow with hope by the power of the Holy Spirit."

Chapter 16

PURPOSE AND PEACE

As we wind down these ABCs of God's promises, I can honestly say that I have discovered my purpose and found profound peace in the process. Growing up, I always felt a bit different; I was often labeled the "problem child," the one who was a smarty-pants and a fighter. I possessed a unique gift that I didn't fully understand, and as I transitioned into young adulthood, that gift became more pronounced. However, fear held me back. I hesitated to share what I felt called to express, thinking, "Who am I to tell you about yourself when you don't even know me?" This reluctance meant I wasn't being obedient to the calling God had placed on my life.

In my journey of healing, restoration, and transformation, I began to understand that my purpose extends far beyond merely prophesying or giving advice. The endurance I cultivated through years of challenges has become my testimony, and that testimony is my ministry. I experienced profound loss as a child, losing my parents at a young age and later facing homelessness. I lived a tumultuous life, filled with bad decisions—fighting, dating drug dealers, and constantly struggling to survive. I witnessed family members battling addiction and experienced the weight of life's harsh realities. It felt as though I had lived through every hardship, and when others approached me with their problems, I could say, "Oh, I've been through that. I lived that. I experienced that."

Yet, in sharing my story, I often failed to give God the glory, mistakenly believing that my own strength was what led me out of darkness. It wasn't until my spiritual journey deepened that I recognized how God had guided me through every trial, enabling me to survive and become more than a conqueror. Now, I have the opportunity to minister from a place of authenticity, sharing how God saved my life and how surrendering to Him transformed my existence.

This realization has culminated in the establishment of my Holy Healing Talk ministry, where I share my purpose while simultaneously experiencing God's peace. In August 2024, I faced significant hardships that tested this newfound peace. I had to call my mortgage company to request a three-month deferment, during which time my son and daughter both lost their jobs. The only steady income came from my oldest daughter, a registered nurse, whose paycheck was not enough to cover the mortgage, which stood at $3,500. Meanwhile, my other son had moved out, leaving us in a precarious situation.

Despite these challenges, my daughter has been able to contribute $500 monthly to help with credit card bills, while my businesses, which had faced setbacks, were slowly recovering. From January to October 2024, I went without a paycheck, relying on credit cards to cover my car payments and other expenses. Yet, in the midst of this financial stress, I found peace. The math of our situation was daunting, but I held onto the knowledge that God has always been my protector and provider.

Even after ten months without a paycheck—facing a mortgage, car payments, insurance, groceries, and utility bills—I remained untroubled. I didn't dwell on the financial strain because I was enveloped in God's peace. I had entrusted my burdens to Him, believing wholeheartedly that He would take care of everything. This peace is what I wish everyone could experience—living in the world while free from depression, anxiety, and the burdens of life. When you surrender everything to God and cast all your cares upon Him, you find solace and rest, allowing Him to handle the details.

Now, I not only know my purpose, but I am also living in peace, fully confident that God is turning my circumstances around for my good. This journey has taught me that while life may present challenges, it is through faith and submission to God that we can find true peace, knowing that He has a plan for us. Each day is a testament to His faithfulness, and I am excited to continue walking in this purpose, sharing the love and grace of God with others who may be navigating their own struggles.

Chapter 17

QUIETNESS

This chapter is indeed quite self-explanatory, yet it carries profound depth. God's promise to me was a call to embrace quietness—an invitation to silence not only my surroundings but also the whirlwind of thoughts in my mind. He urged me to simply be still and to cultivate a space of tranquility where I could truly hear Him. In a world filled with noise and distractions, it's easy to get caught up in our own chatter, drowning out the gentle whispers of the Divine. When we talk too much and too loudly, we risk pushing ourselves further away from the blessings and rewards that await us at the finish line of our journey.

Through this divine lesson, I learned the importance of being quiet, of knowing when to speak and when to listen. It's a practice that requires discipline and trust—trusting that God's timing is perfect and that He will guide me when I am still. I've come to see myself as a beautiful art piece that was once broken but has been lovingly restored by the Creator. This restoration process has been deeply intertwined with my ability to embrace quietness, which I now understand as a form of spiritual isolation—a sacred space where I can focus solely on my relationship with God.

When I pray, I communicate my needs, desires, praises, gratitude, and, most importantly, my love for Him. Prayer is my way of reaching out, of expressing everything that weighs on my heart. However, I've learned that prayer is only one side of the conversation. In moments of quiet, I engage in meditation, allowing myself to listen deeply for God's voice. It's in this stillness that I can truly absorb His wisdom and guidance.

Giving God time to speak to me has been transformative. I've discovered that He often answers in subtle ways—a thought that arises, a feeling of peace, or a verse that resonates with my current situation. The more I practice quietness, the more attuned I become to His presence, and the clearer His direction becomes in my life. It's a beautiful exchange, one that deepens my faith and enriches my understanding of His love for me.

In our fast-paced world, the art of quietness can feel like a luxury, but it is, in fact, a necessity for spiritual growth. When we take the time to be quiet, we open ourselves up to receive the profound insights God wishes to share with us. We create an environment where His promises can unfold, where we can feel His peace wash over us, and where we can find clarity amidst the chaos. So, let us not underestimate the power of being still. Embrace the quiet, and you may find that God has been waiting for you there, ready to guide you toward the rewards He has in store.

COLOSSIANS
1:11

"May you be strengthened with all power according to his glorious might so that you may have great endurance and patience."

Chapter 18

RIGHTEOUSNESS

Living righteously is an essential part of my journey, one that has been deeply shaped by my relationship with God. I've come to understand that righteousness is not just a set of rules to follow but a way of embodying God's Word in everything I do. I acknowledge that I am not perfect, and that realization is crucial. Each morning, the first thing I do upon waking is to thank the Holy Spirit for the gift of a new day, for the breath in my lungs, and for the opportunity to make things right.

I know that many of us have our morning routines— some begin with prayer before rising from bed. Yet, I also admit that there are mornings when I drop the ball. There are times when I instinctively reach for my phone and scroll through social media instead of centering myself in prayer or reflection. In those moments, I practice repentance, seeking God's understanding of my heart's true desires. I want Him to know that my intention is to be more like Him, to align my actions with His will.

It's important to remember that we have all adapted to worldly ways. God understands this struggle, which is why He has reassured us that the path to righteousness won't be easy, but it will be worth the effort. Many of the habits we cling to are ingrained in us from birth, shaped by our environments and experiences. However, as I strive to get closer to God, I've learned that He knows my heart. Choosing to be righteous is not just for the sake of appearances or to please others; it is a personal commitment to live in alignment with my true self.

Throughout my journey, I have actively sought to embody righteousness in tangible ways. One specific prayer I offered was for God to change my speech; I wanted to break the habit of swearing. And He did. I also struggled with smoking for 20 years, and as part of my commitment to living righteously and taking better care of my temple, I asked God for help. Remarkably, I have been smoke-free for two years, a testament to God's transformative power in my life.

God's righteousness is evident in how He guides me to correct my path. To fully embody His Word and serve as an example of His love, I must strive to live right. I understand that I cannot fulfill the purpose He has laid out for me if I am not aligned with His truth. It's a continuous journey, and while I may not always get it right, I know that God sees my heart and my efforts to improve.

There are still those in my life who may only see my past mistakes or my fleshly ways, refusing to acknowledge the spiritual growth I've undergone since surrendering my life to God. But their perception does not deter me. My role is to keep pushing forward, to walk in God's Word, and to be a living testament of His righteousness. I trust that God will handle their perspectives while He continues to nurture my growth.

Striving for righteousness is about establishing a deep, authentic relationship with God. It's about being real with Him and trusting that He knows the sincerity of my heart. As I work to get closer to Him, I realize that this journey is not just about me; it's about how I can reflect His love and grace to those around me. In doing so, I find peace in knowing that God is with me every step of the way, guiding me, teaching me, and helping me become the person I was always meant to be.

HEBREWS
6:19

"We have this hope as an anchor for the soul, firm and secure."

Chapter 19

SAVED & SAFE

I vividly remember the moment God saved my soul, when He lifted away the heavy burden of worldly emotions that the enemy relentlessly attacks me with each day. It felt as if God was performing a profound reset in my life, breathing new life into me—air that I had never inhaled before. In that transformative moment, I discovered clarity in my vision; it was as though a veil had been lifted, allowing me to truly see the beauty and purpose in my life. My hearing sharpened, and I began to perceive things differently—sounds of joy, hope, and truth resonated in a way that was previously muted.

My communication with God took on a new depth; my praises flowed effortlessly, almost on automatic mode. My prayers transformed, infused with a sincerity and fervor that I had never experienced. As I looked at myself in the mirror, I saw a glow radiating from within—a reflection of the internal change that God had orchestrated. The smile that adorned my face was genuine, organic, and completely natural; it was no longer forced or fake. For the first time in my life, I not only felt saved but also truly safe.

This newfound sense of safety was empowering. I felt untouchable, shielded from the influences and temptations that once had easy access to my heart. The desires of the world, which had previously captivated me, lost their allure. I used to ask for everything on my birthdays—not simply out of necessity, but from a place of wanting. Material possessions provided me with a fleeting sense of comfort and security, as if owning them meant they were mine and no one could take them away.

But then God intervened. He opened my eyes to the reality that people, places, and things in this world are transient—they do not last forever. In contrast, the promise of eternal life with God is a treasure that cannot be taken away. This revelation shifted my perspective profoundly. I learned to hold onto His Word—the very Word that saved me and continues to make me feel safe.

The Scriptures became my refuge, a source of strength and assurance in times of uncertainty. Each promise reassured me that I am protected and loved beyond measure. I found solace in knowing that God is my fortress, my safe haven amidst life's storms. It is this relationship with Him that grants me true security, far beyond the temporary comforts I once sought in the world.

Now, I approach life with a renewed sense of purpose, anchored in the knowledge that my worth is not found in material things but in my identity as a child of God. I am reminded daily that I am saved and safe, and that truth empowers me to navigate life with confidence, joy, and peace. By embracing this new reality, I am free to live fully and authentically, sharing the love and light of Christ with those around me, knowing that true safety lies in His embrace.

PSALM 16:8

"I keep my eyes always on the Lord. With him at my right hand, I will not be shaken."

Chapter 20

TRUTH

John 14:6 proclaims, "I am the way, the truth, and the life." These powerful words resonate deeply within me, encapsulating everything I need to understand about my relationship with God. When I first encountered this verse, I felt as though God had spoken directly to my heart. "Say no more, say no less," it seemed to convey. This singular statement is profound in its simplicity, yet it holds the weight of divine truth that can transform lives.

Reflecting on my past, I often wish I had discovered this truth years earlier. How different my journey might have been if I had grasped the significance of these words sooner! In a world filled with confusion, distractions, and competing narratives, the assurance that Jesus is the embodiment of truth is both liberating and grounding. He doesn't just point the way; He is the way. He doesn't merely share truths; He is the truth. And He doesn't offer life as a concept; He is the very essence of life itself.

This revelation is a promise that God has been unfolding in my life every day. Each morning, I wake up with the knowledge that I can rely on Him as my guiding light. In moments of uncertainty, when the world seems to spin out of control, I remind myself that I have a steadfast anchor in Christ. He provides clarity amid chaos, direction in times of indecision, and life where there was once despair.

As I reflect on my spiritual journey, I realize that this promise is not just about intellectual acknowledgment; it is about living in alignment with the truth of who Jesus is. This truth calls me to a deeper relationship with Him, urging me to seek His guidance in every aspect of my life. When I face challenges, I can turn to Him for wisdom and understanding. When I feel lost or uncertain, I can rest in the assurance that He knows the path I should take.

Moreover, embracing this truth means that I am also called to share it with others. In a society that often grapples with relativism and uncertainty, I feel a responsibility to illuminate the way for those around me. By embodying the truth of Christ in my actions and words, I can be a light in the darkness, guiding others toward the hope and life that can be found in Him.

Ultimately, John 14:6 serves as a constant reminder of the promises that God has for me. It reassures me that I am not navigating this journey alone; I have a Savior who is intimately involved in my life, providing me with the way, the truth, and the life I so desperately need. My heart is filled with gratitude for this promise, and I am committed to living each day in the light of His truth, trusting that He will continue to reveal Himself to me in new and profound ways.

JOSHUA 1:9

"Have I not commanded you? Be strong and courageous. Do not be frightened, and do not be dismayed, for the LORD your God is with you wherever you go."

Chapter 21

UNITY

As we navigate the unbearable burdens of loss, pain, and emotional hurt from experiences of abandonment and trauma, it's common to feel isolated and alone. When these feelings persist over time, they can manifest into social anxiety, often without us even realizing it. I faced a multitude of challenges that contributed to my own social anxiety, despite being raised in a family and having friends around me. In a world that sometimes feels overwhelmingly lonely, I found myself in a mental state where I felt the need to protect myself at all costs. This led to discomfort and unease around people I genuinely wanted to connect with, but my mind often told me to retreat.

This was not a spiritual separation but rather a mental isolation I had imposed on myself. I allowed anxieties, depression, and the habit of overthinking to keep me distant from the very people I loved. I didn't want to be a burden to anyone, so I pushed through my struggles, mistakenly believing I was carving out a path for myself and my children. In reality, it was God who was making a way for me, guiding me toward healing and connection.

Once I surrendered my life to Christ, everything changed. I began to experience the joy of being around people who didn't judge me, who genuinely wanted to pray for me, encourage me, and uplift me. These individuals empowered me and reminded me that I am still a beloved child of God. In this newfound community, I recognized the profound unity among God's children.

I learned that family is not solely defined by blood relations; it can also be forged through meaningful connections with those whom God intentionally places in our lives. I have encountered relationships with people who were divinely appointed to support me in my time of need. God revealed to me that the unity among His children is vital; we are called to pour into one another, to uplift and encourage each other as we navigate this often-chaotic world.

The Bible echoes this sentiment in 1 Corinthians 1:10, where it states, "I appeal to you, brothers and sisters, in the name of our Lord Jesus Christ, that all of you agree with one another in what you say and that there be no divisions among you, but that you be perfectly united in mind and thought." This scripture has taught me the importance of alignment with God's purpose. When we stand together, united in spirit and intent, we create a powerful force for good in our lives and the lives of others.

While we may not be able to take everyone along on our journeys, we can commit to continuous prayer and unwavering support for one another, especially during times of need. This unity fosters an environment where we can all thrive, reminding us that we are never truly alone. We are a community, bound together by faith, love, and a shared purpose, and in that unity, we find strength, healing, and hope. Together, we can face the challenges of life, uplift one another in our struggles, and celebrate the victories that come from being aligned with God's will.

ROMANS
8:28

"And we know that for those who love God all things work together for good, for those who are called according to His purpose."

Chapter 22

VICTORIOUS

Experiencing God in my life has profoundly transformed my understanding of victory. I have come to realize just how much power I hold over the enemy and the myriads of challenges he attempts to throw my way. Reflecting on my ten-month living situation, I can confidently proclaim that God has already granted me victory over that struggle. I have triumphed over broken relationships, and I have emerged victorious from the shadows of homelessness. Each of these experiences has been a testament to God's unwavering presence and His promise that I can overcome any obstacle with Him by my side.

God has shown me that, with Him, I can defy all odds. The popular saying goes, "Today we ate and left no crumbs," and I embody that sentiment. I am a victorious woman of God, and I declare this truth proudly, boldly, and with the authority that comes from my faith. The journey to this realization has not been easy; it has taken time, perseverance, and a deep commitment to trusting in God's plan for my life.

No devil, whether near or far, can come between me and my Father. I refuse to allow any negativity or doubt to infiltrate my spirit. The victory I carry within me is not just a feeling; it's a reality that envelops my life. I am fortified by the knowledge that the enemy has no access to me. God's protection surrounds me, creating a barrier that shields me from his attacks.

This sense of victory permeates every aspect of my life. It empowers me to face challenges with confidence and resilience, knowing that I am not fighting alone. As I navigate hardships, I remind myself that each trial is an opportunity for growth and a chance to witness God's power at work. My faith is not just a personal journey; it's a declaration of strength that can inspire others to seek their own victories.

In sharing my story, I hope to encourage those who may be feeling defeated or trapped in their circumstances. Victory is not reserved for the few; it is available to anyone who chooses to walk in faith and trust in God's promises. Together, we can rise above the struggles, knowing that we are equipped to conquer whatever the enemy throws our way.

I stand firm in my identity as a victorious woman of God, embracing the life He has given me with gratitude and joy. Each day is a new opportunity to demonstrate how God's grace and strength can lead us through the darkness into the light. I am determined to live out this victory, sharing it with others and shining a light on the path toward freedom. In doing so, I affirm that with God, we are always victorious.

PSALM 121:1-2

"I lift up my eyes to the hills. From where does my help come? My help comes from the LORD, who made heaven and earth."

Chapter 23

WONDERFULLY MADE

God has profoundly taught me about my identity and worth through His Word, embedding the truth so deeply in my mind and spirit that it has become an inseparable part of who I am. The scripture from Psalms 139:14 resonates within me: "I will praise you, for I am fearfully and wonderfully made." This powerful affirmation serves as a constant reminder of my unique value and the divine craftsmanship that went into creating me.

Understanding that I am made in the image of God fills me with awe and gratitude. It means that I am not just a random collection of traits or a mere product of chance; I am a deliberate and intentional creation, designed with purpose and love. This realization transforms the way I view myself and how I interact with the world around me. Each characteristic, flaw, and strength is part of a greater design, meant to reflect God's glory and to fulfill a specific role in His grand plan.

Recognizing that I am "fearfully and wonderfully made" compels me to represent God well in every aspect of my life. It instills in me a sense of responsibility to honor my Creator by embracing my uniqueness and living authentically. I am called not only to appreciate my own worth but also to encourage others to see their own value as God's creations. This perspective shifts the focus from comparison and insecurity to celebration and empowerment.

I strive to embody the love and grace that God has shown me, understanding that my actions and words should reflect His character. When I encounter challenges or moments of self-doubt, I return to this scripture as a source of strength and affirmation. It reminds me that I am equipped with everything I need to navigate life's trials, because I am wonderfully made, crafted with intention and care by the Creator of the universe.

Moreover, this understanding encourages me to cultivate a deeper relationship with God. I seek to learn more about His nature and how I can align my life with His purpose. By doing so, I not only honor myself but also glorify Him. Each day becomes an opportunity to praise Him for His incredible work in creating me and to share that message of affirmation with others.

In a world where so many struggle with feelings of inadequacy, I find it particularly important to spread the message that we are all wonderfully made. This truth has the power to heal, uplift, and inspire. It can break the chains of self-doubt and lead individuals to embrace their unique identities. Together, we can celebrate the beauty of our differences and recognize that we are all part of a divine tapestry, each thread meticulously woven together by God's hand.

So let us hold onto the truth that we are fearfully and wonderfully made, and let it inspire us to live fully and authentically, representing God in all that we do. In doing so, we not only honor our own journeys but also reflect the brilliance of our Creator to the world around us.

JOHN 16:33

"In the world you will have tribulation. But take heart; I have overcome the world."

Chapter 24

(E) XCELLENT

In every aspect of our spiritual journey, God is dedicated to training and maturing His children. He desires that we utilize every bit of His wisdom and knowledge, even when circumstances might not make sense to those around us. Trusting in His understanding is paramount, which is why immersing ourselves in His Word is so vital. As I reflected on my own spiritual journey, I found myself asking God for a word that starts with the letter "X," something that encapsulates how He has trained and matured me.

At first, I struggled to find a suitable word, but then I felt the Spirit guiding me to look beyond the constraints of the alphabet. God gently reminded me that while there may not be many words that begin with "X," there are certainly many that carry the "X" sound or embody His essence. In this moment of contemplation, I opened my Bible and engaged in a heartfelt conversation with God, seeking His guidance on how to complete the alphabet of promises He has bestowed upon me.

As I continued this dialogue, I was led to Psalm 150:2, specifically in the King James Version: "Praise him according to his excellent greatness." This verse resonated deeply within me, reinforcing the message that God wanted me to grasp. He was reminding me of His excellence, urging me to acknowledge that while my journey might not always align with what I see, it is grounded in faith and what I hear from Him. Our God is indeed an excellent God, deserving of praise that reflects His magnificent greatness.

In this moment of clarity, I found myself expressing gratitude to God. I declared, "You are great, you are good, you are amazing!" These words flowed from my heart as I recognized the depth of His love and the richness of His character. I closed my eyes and felt an overwhelming sense of connection, knowing that He was providing me with the words I needed to articulate my experiences and complete this chapter of my life.

This journey of faith is not just about the milestones we achieve but also about the continuous preparation for the next level God is taking us to. Every challenge, every lesson, and every moment of growth is an opportunity to praise Him for His excellent greatness. Therefore, I am reminded to make it a daily practice to give God all the glory, to celebrate His presence in my life, and to acknowledge the many ways He is working behind the scenes.

As I move forward, I commit to praising God at every turn—whether in moments of joy or in times of struggle. I want to honor His greatness not only in my words but also in my actions. Each day presents a new opportunity to recognize the excellence of our Creator and the incredible ways He shapes our lives. So let us remember to uplift His name, for He is deserving of our praise, and let us share the testimony of His goodness and greatness with others, inspiring them to see the beauty of walking by faith.

PROVERBS
3:5-6

"Trust in the LORD with all your heart, and do not lean on your own understanding. In all your ways acknowledge Him, and He will make straight your paths."

Chapter 25

YIELD

As I've discussed in earlier segments of this book, the journey toward experiencing love, peace, joy, comfort, care, faith, blessings, and abundance began with a profound act of surrender. Before I could embark on this transformative journey of healing, I had to relinquish my entire life—my soul, my heart, and my mind—over to Christ. This surrender was not merely a gesture; it was an essential step that enabled me to cultivate a strong, healthy relationship with Jesus Christ, our Savior. The act of yielding required me to let go of my own desires and give God all of me, creating space for His divine purpose to unfold in my life.

To truly yield, I had to decrease myself so that God could increase within me. This is a critical aspect of spiritual growth—understanding that we cannot bring our old selves, along with our baggage, into this new life that God offers. When we hold onto even a small part of our past or the toxic elements that weigh us down, we hinder the beautiful transformation God has in store for us. When God asks if we are ready to embrace this new beginning, our affirmative response must come with the readiness to completely let go.

Initially, my journey was anything but smooth. It started off rocky because I didn't yield fully to God. I surrendered enough to feel comfortable, yet I clung to certain aspects of my life that I thought I could manage. This led to days and nights filled with struggle, where my discomfort turned into weeks and then months of turmoil. I was inadvertently dragging remnants of toxicity into the sacred space God had blessed me with. I realized that my desire for comfort was holding me back from experiencing the true comfort that God had waiting for me.

In those moments, I cried out in fear, grappling with the uncertainty of letting go. Yet, the more I sought God, the more I understood that I couldn't trust the fleeting things I could see. Instead, I felt a profound sense of safety when I closed my eyes and tuned into the goodness of God within me. This realization propelled me to completely let go and yield to Him.

Trust me, as I write these words, I acknowledge that this process was not easy. The journey of yielding, the act of surrendering—none of it came without its challenges. But I stand here today to affirm that every struggle was worth it. In surrendering, I discovered a deeper connection with God that I had never experienced before. It became a sacred space where it was just me and God, free from the burdens of the world. I learned to pray and trust God to take care of everything in my life.

The worldly burdens I once carried felt like weights on my shoulders, threatening to sabotage my happiness and purpose. I never want to experience that overwhelming feeling again. While I may not have faced the same hardships as some of you, I encourage you to reflect on this question: if you could hand everything off to one person you trust, who would that be? For me, the answer is unequivocally God.

So, let us embrace the act of yielding, knowing that it opens the door to a life of purpose, joy, and divine connection with our Creator.

JAMES 1:2-3

"Consider it pure joy, my brothers and sisters, whenever you face trials of many kinds, because you know that the testing of your faith produces perseverance."

Chapter 26

ZEALOUS

As we reach the end of the alphabet of God's promises, I am filled with a sense of urgency and excitement to share this journey with you all. God has been revealing these truths to me over time, and with each new word, I felt a stirring in my spirit. It became clear that it was finally time to put pen to paper and release these insights into the world. I am in a new season of elevation with God, and I can no longer hold onto these revelations. My hope is that as I share these ABCs of God's promises, they will resonate deeply, pierce the hearts of many, and ultimately save some souls—just as they have saved my own.

To be zealous means to be filled with passion and enthusiasm for something, and I am genuinely excited about my relationship with God. I am enthused by His Word and the profound truths contained within it. The teachings I have received during this time of growth and maturation have been transformative, guiding me to live out my purpose and embrace my position in His kingdom. I have learned to enjoy the peace that comes from aligning my life with His will, and it fills me with a zealous spirit.

In Revelation 3:19, the scripture states, "As many as I love, I rebuke and chasten. Be zealous, therefore, and repent." This passage resonates with me deeply. In the past, I often apologized for my mistakes, quickly uttering "I'm sorry" without fully understanding the weight of my actions. However, I realized that merely saying I'm sorry can sometimes open the door for the same mistakes to occur repeatedly. God called me to a higher level of accountability, urging me to grow and mature beyond superficial apologies.

I learned that my actions needed to align with my words. So, I made it a personal commitment to work diligently to avoid repeating my past mistakes. When I do falter, I am swift to repent—not just as a ritual, but as a genuine act of contrition and desire for growth. I have adopted the practice of repenting first thing in the morning and throughout the day, addressing both the known and unknown shortcomings in my life. My repentance is filled with zeal because I am confident that God hears me and values my sincere desire to improve.

As believers, it is crucial that our actions align with the teachings of God's Word. It's not enough to simply believe; we must embody that belief through our daily lives. We need to be believers who walk the walk and talk the talk, ensuring our lives reflect God's truth and love. Embracing this zealousness for the Gospel means actively living out our faith, sharing His love with others, and demonstrating the transformative power of His grace.

This journey has taught me that zealousness is not just about excitement; it's about commitment and integrity. It's about being passionate enough to hold myself accountable and to strive for a life that honors God in every way. As I continue to walk this path, I encourage you to join me in being zealous—let's dive deeper into our relationship with God and allow His promises to guide us. Together, we can be a shining example of His love and truth in a world that desperately needs it.

Made in the USA
Columbia, SC
25 October 2024

44715345R00059